Jeffrey Plowman

CAMOUFLAGE & MARKINGS
of
German Armor
in Italy

From Anzio Landing to the Alps
January 1944 – May 1945

Model Centrum PROGRES

Armor Color Gallery #17

Camouflage & Markings of
German Armor in Italy
From Anzio Landing to the Alps
January 1944 – May 1945

Jeffrey Plowman

Published by Model Centrum Progres, Poland
Warsaw, January 2022

ISBN 978-83-60672-35-8

Edited by Wojciech J. Gawrych
Cover layout, design and layout by
PROGRES Publishing House, Warsaw
DTP and prepress by Liwia Morawska
Printed and bound in European Union by
REGIS Ltd., Napoleona 4, 05-230 Kobyłka,
Poland

First Edition

Exclusive Distributor
Model Centrum
Warsaw, Poland
wjg-books@wp.pl

Contents

Acknowledgments

I grateful to the following veterans gave me access to the photographs of these that appear in this book: E. Anderson, Roy Arnold, Ron Burton, Pat Gourdie, Ben Hoban, Keith Jarman, Ray McFarlane, Jock Montgomery, Jim Moodie, Nigel Ogle, Eric Round, Arthur Smith, Des Tomkies and Allan Williamson. I also wish to thank the following people who supplied photographs and assisted me with information on camouflage and markings: Lee Archer, Marco Dalmonte, Wojciech J. Gawrych, Stefano di Giusto, Nicolaus Hettler (Nuts & Bolts), John Nicholson, Brendon O'Carroll and Stuart Smith. My thanks also to the following organisations for the use of their photographs: the Alexander Turnbull Library [ATL], the Imperial War Museum [IWM], the National Army Museum NZ [NAMNZ], the US National Archives and Records Administration [NARA], the Polish Institute and Sikorski Museum [PISM], Narodowe Archiwum Cyfrowe [NAC], Real War Photos [RWP], the Tank Museum at Bovington [TMB], the South African Defence Force [SADF] archives and the US Army Heritage and Education Centre [USAHEC].

German plans to defend Italy against an invasion by the Allies were based on the view of Generalfeldmarschall Albert Kesselring, commander of Heeresgruppe C, that it would be possible to hold Rome until at least the summer of 1944. To achieve this he established a series of defensive lines up the peninsula, the first of these being the Viktor Line running along the line of the Volturno and Biferno rivers in the west to Termoli on the Adriatic Coast. Beyond this lay the Barbara Line and then the Bernhardt Line, the latter running along the Garigliano river before turning inland to San Severo and thence to Ortona on the Adriatic Coast. To further strengthen this position Kesselring established a switch line, the Gustav Line, this one running from the Bernhardt Line inland through Monte Cassino. Beyond this was the Hitler Line, which crossed the Liri valley from Pontecorvo to Piedmonte San Germano.

The Allies reached the Bernhardt Line at the end of 1943 at the point where the Garigliano river reached the sea. It was here, in late January 1944, that the British launched their first attack, primarily to draw off German units from the area around Rome prior to the Allied landings at Anzio and Nettuno. Next the Allies launched a series of attacks on the Gustav Line proper, the first across the Gari river around Sant'Angelo in Theodice and then three more on Monte Cassino and the town of Cassino below it. Finally on 11 May 1944 the Allies launched Operation Diadem, a broad thrust from the sea to Monte Cassino that saw them finally break through the line seven days later, after which they drove on towards the Hitler/Senger Line, penetrating this and striking out to link up with the troops at Anzio.

On 2 May 1945 Panzer-Abteilung 212 attempted to cross the Austrian border to escape the advancing British forces. A few kilometres to the north near Gemona it would run into a British column, destroying several Staghound armoured cars and other vehicles in the resulting clash. This PzKpfw III Ausf. N "Erika" passing through Buia, north of Gemona, appears to be completed in a two- or three-tone disruptive scheme over the Zimmerit paste on its armour. [Stefano di Giusto]

On 3 June 1944 Panther Ausf. A, number 425, from 4. Kompanie, Panzer-Regiment 26, broke down because of lack of fuel and spare parts near Fuggi while retreating north from Lazio. It appears to have been completed in overall Dunkelgelb, with its gun barrel camouflaged in Olivgrün and Rotbraun. The tactical number in red outlined in white. [Jeffrey Plowman]

Leutnant Kockert's Panther Ausf. A, number 433, from 4. Kompanie, Panzer-Regiment 26, was knocked out on 24 May 1944 after destroying nine enemy tanks. It was most probably completed in Dunkelgelb, oversprayed with Olivgrün, with the number in red outlined with white. [John Nicholson]

[Previous page & above] Panzer-Regiment 26 was forced to abandon this early model Panther Ausf. A, number 202, in Fontana Liri through track failure. It appears to have been completed in overall Dunkelgelb, with the tactical number in red outlined in white. [Des Tomkies; Stuart Smith; Brendon O'Carroll]

Among the equipment abandoned by the Axis during their retreat north was this Semovente da 47/32. It was completed in overall Dunkelgelb. [John Nicholson]

Among vehicles abandoned in the Liri valley was this M42 75/34 851(i). It is completed in a two-tone scheme of either Olivgrün or Rotbraun over Dunkelgelb. [Jeffrey Plowman]

Track failure seems to have been a common problem for Panzer-Regiment 26 during their retreat up the Melfa valley, this Panther Ausf. A, number 423, from 4. Kompanie, being abandoned through this after destroying two Shermans during an Allied counter-attack on 24 May 1944. It appears to have been completed in overall Dunkelgelb, with the tactical number in red outlined in white. [Jock Montgomery]

Operation Shingle, the amphibious landing at Anzio-Nettuno, was first conceived by the British Prime Minister, Winston Churchill, as a way to outflank the Gustav Line and secure Rome. Its timing was based on the limited availability of landing craft, which would soon be needed for the invasion in northern France. The operation was entrusted to Major-General John P. Lucas, commander of the US VI Corps. Launched on 22 January 1944, it initially achieved complete surprise, capturing both Anzio and Nettuno before penetrating a further two miles inland, a jeep patrol actually reaching as far as the outskirts of Rome. Unfortunately, Lucas failed to capitalise on this, choosing instead to build up his forces at the beachhead before driving further inland. Kesselring, however, had prepared for this, his divisions having established motorised rapid reaction units specifically to deal swiftly with this type of situation. Within hours of the Allied landings, battlegroups from both 4. Fallschirmjäger-Division and the Herman Göring Panzer-Division took control of the roads leading into the Alban hills from Anzio. This they held until another 20,000 troops reached the area that evening. In the meantime requests for more troops were sent to Oberkommando der Wehrmacht, resulting in some being diverted from the Gothic Line to the north. Within three days Kesselring had placed a ring around Lucas' troops, the German control of the hills giving them good observation for artillery fire on the beachhead. To compound the Allies' problems the Germans turned off the drainage pumps in the valley below and flooded what had formerly been the Pontine marshes.

Lucas launched his first attack on 30 January, but the British failed to take Campoleone and ended up in a salient along the Via Anziate. The Americans, however, managed to push forward three miles towards Cisterna. The Germans responded with a series of counterattacks on the Campoleone salient, starting

Panzer-Kompanie Meyer was sent to Northern Italy in July 1943 as part of the hurried deployment of troops to bolster German forces there. The unit eventually reached Balzano in August of that year where this early model Tiger I was photographed. At this stage of the war it was completed in Dunkelgelb. [NAC]

The next deployment of Panzer-Kompanie Meyer was Anzio at the end of January 1944, but by now the base coat of the tanks had been over-sprayed with Olivgrün and Rotbrun. This Tiger I also carries the name "Strolch" (drifter) on the driver's front plate, its unit insignia, a Balten-kreuzschild, on its transmission front plate and the identification number 8 on the side of the turret. [NAC]

The next Tiger unit to arrive in Italy was schwere Panzer-Abteilung 508, unloading their tanks at Ficulle-Fab-rio, the crew of Tiger 113 being pho-tographed changing over from their transport to combat tracks. It was completed in a disruptive scheme of Olivgrün and Rotbrun over its base coat of Dunkelgelb, with the unit in-signia of a black charging bison on the side of the turret bin. Character-istic of the unit at this time was the fact that the second two numbers are smaller than the first.

on 3 February and continuing to the 16th, by which time the Allies had been forced back to the line of their original beachhead. By 20 February this attack had run its course, an attack by VI Corps bringing it to an end. At Adolf Hitler's insistence a further attack was launched on 29 February, but this achieved little. Realising that no decisive result could be achieved until Spring, the battlefield slipped into a period of stalemate whereby both sides maintained vigorous patrolling and artillery duels, while setting about to rebuild their respective forces, VI Corps, now under Major-General Lucian Truscott, preparing for Operation Diadem, the breakout from the Gustav Line.

On the morning of 23 May, following the Allied breakout from Cassino and the attack on the Hitler Line, Truscott launched an attack with the aim of breaking through the German defences around Anzio-Netuno. This took the form of a feint up the Via Anziate towards Rome, with the primary thrust towards Valmontone to cut off the retreat of X. Armee from Cassino. However, on the evening of 25 May, with American troops heading into the Velletri gap, the US Fifth Army commander, General Mark Clark, ordered the weight of the attack to be shifted towards Rome. This involved the realignment of a number of units from VI Corps and while this was happening Kesselring threw four divisions into the Veletri Gap, holding it for four days, allowing seven divisions from X. Armee to withdraw through to Rome. In the meantime the main VI Corps thrust along the Via Anziate met with strong German resistance until 30 May. At this point the Allies broke through the Caesar Line, threatening Velletri from the rear. Two days later the Caesar Line collapsed and the Germans fell back on Rome, the Americans entering the city on 4 June.

[This page] One of the responsibilities of 3. Kompanie, schwere Panzer-Abteilung 508, was that of operating the schwere Ladungsträger (SdKfz 301) demolition vehicles, controlled by these PzKpfw III Ausf. H or J tanks. They appear to be completed in Dunkelgelb overpainted with Olivgrün, and Rotbrun. [Jeffrey Plowman]

[*This page*] In February 1944 Panther tanks from I. Abteilung, Panzer-Regiment 26, arrived in Rome, this early production Panther Ausf. A, number 215, from 2. Kompanie, being photographed on the Via dell'Imperio. It was completed in overall Dunkelgelb with red turret numbers outlined in white.

This Tiger I from schwere Panzer-Abteilung 508 was also photographed passing through Rome on its way south to Anzio-Netuno. It appears to be completed in Dunkelgelb oversprayed with Olivgrün and Rotbrun.

Panther Ausf. A (early production), number I14, from 1. Kompanie, I. Abteilung, Panzer-Regiment 26, was also photographed on the Via dell'Imperio. It was completed in overall Dunkelgelb with red turret numbers outlined in white.

After departing Ficulle-Fabrio schwere Panzer-Abteilung 508 set off south by road for Rome reaching it early in February 1944, this Tiger I being photographed driving past the National Monument to Victor Emmanuel II. It was completed in Dunkelgelb oversprayed with Olivgrün and Rotbrun.

[This page] After leaving Rome Tiger I number 134 from schwere Panzer-Abteilung 508 set off along the Via Appia towards Isola Bella. WIt was completed in Dunkelgelb oversprayed with Olivgrün and Rotbrun, with the turret numbers in white.

[*This page*] The crew of this Tiger I from 2 Kompanie, schwere Panzer-Abteilung 508, are in the process of replacing its track. It was completed in Dunkelgelb oversprayed with Olivgrün and Rotbrun, with the turret numbers in white. [RWP]

This Panther Ausf. A from I. Abteilung, Panzer-Regiment 26 was photographed on the road to Cisterna. It was completed in overall Dunkelgelb. The turret numbers, of which only 3 is clearly visible, would be red outlined in white.

[Right & below right] The Germans brought forward other units to the Anzio-Nettuno front, this column of StuG IIIs photographed passing through Rome on their way south. They appear to be completed in overall Dunkelgelb.

Employed as a Befehls-Panther, this Ausf. D from I. Abteilung, Panzer-Regiment 26, is heading south on the road to Cisterna. It was completed in overall Dunkelgelb.

After taking Carroceta outside Aprilia on 3 March 1944, 3. Panzergrenadier-Division moved these two Grilles (15 cm Schweres Infanteriegeschütze 33 (Sf) auf Pzkpfw 38(t) Ausf. H) into its ruins to use them in a fire support role. The Grille in front is completed in a Dunkelgelb base coat been over-sprayed with Olivgrün. [NAC]

This Sturmpanzer 43 from Sturm-panzer-Abteilung 216 was photo-graphed in Cisterna. It appears to have been completed in Dunkelgelb oversprayed with web-like pattern of Olivgrün. The vehicle in the fore-ground carries the number 2 behind the Balkenkreuz on the side armour. [Marco Dalmonte]

Sturmpanzer 43s from Sturmpanzer-Abteilung 216 at Anzio appear to have been completed in a variety of cam-ouflage schemes, this one in Dun-kelgelb oversprayed with a web-like pattern of Olivgrün. [NAC]

A line of captured British and American troops pass a PzKpfw II and a Sturmpanzer 43 from Sturmpanzer-Abteilung 216 at Anzio. The Sturmpanzer 43 appears to be completed in Dunkelgelb oversprayed with Olivgrün and Rotbrun. The PzKpfw II looks to have been completed in Dunkelgelb oversprayed with Olivgrün. [NAC]

While the crew from schwere Panzer-Abteilung 508 inspect their Tiger I, a Sturmpanzer 43 from Sturmpanzer-Abteilung 216 at Anzio drives past. The Sturmpanzer 43 appears to have been completed in Dunkelgelb oversprayed with web-like pattern of Olivgrün. [NAC]

These two PzKpfw IVs from Panzer-Regiment 26 were abandoned during the fighting at Anzio. The nearest vehicle, an Ausf. H, number 621, appears to be completed in Dunkelgelb oversprayed with wavy stripes of either Olivgrün or Rotbrun, with the turret numbers possibly in black. [RWP]

[Right & below] Elefant, number 102, from 1. Kompanie, schwere Panzer-jäger-Abteilung 653 commanded by its Kompanie commander, Haupt-mann Hellmut Ulbricht, was abandoned between Cisterna and Ceri on 24 May 1944 after its engine caught fire. It appears to be completed in overall Dunkelgelb, with the number 102 in white. The phohotograph in the right was taken later at Aberdeen Proving Ground in the USA. [USAHEC]

During the retreat north from Cassino this PzKpfw IV Ausf. H, number 725, from 7. Kompanie, Panzer-Regiment 26, was abandoned near Sezze. It appears to have been completed in Dunkelgelb oversprayed with stripes of Rotbraun, with turret numbers in red outlined in white. [NARA]

This Elefant, number 113, 1. Kompanie, schwere Panzerjäger-Abteilung 653, was knocked out by USAAF fighter-bombers on Via Aurelia, to the north of Rome on 5 June 1944, killing Obergefreiter Lässig. It appears to be completed in overall Dunkelgelb, the number 113 being white. [Lee Archer]

This Elefant appears to be completed in a three-tone disruptive scheme of Olivgrün and Rotbraun sprayed over Dunkelgelb. [Jeffrey Plowman]

In April 1944 the Germans put on a fire demonstration near Anzio. Among the vehicles taking part were this Panther Ausf. A, number 301, from I. Abteilung, Panzer-Regiment 26, and a StuG III from Panzer-Abteilung 103, 3. Panzergrenadier-Division. The Panther is completed in overall Dunkelgelb and the StuG III in stripes of Olivgrün oversprayed onto Dunkelgelb.

During the retreat from Anzio-Netuno the crew of this StuG III Ausf. G were forced to abandon it near Valmontone. It appears to be completed in Dunkelgelb oversprayed with lines of Olivgrün. [PISM]

American troops found this Sturm-panzer 43 from Sturmpanzer-Abteilung 216 after their entry into Rome. It appears to be completed in Dunkelgelb, oversprayed with Olivgrün, and Rotbrun. [Jeffrey Plowman]

The crew of Elefant, number 124, from 1. Kompanie, schwere Panzer-jäger-Abteilung 653, blew it up in the Piazza Vittorio Emanuele III in Soriano nel Cimino Via Aurelia on 10 June after it suffered mechanical problems. It appears to be completed in overall Dunkelgelb, with the number 124 in white. [NARA]

Retreat to the Apennines

Following the fall of Rome, Allied pressure on the Germans forced them to fall back to a line running from Pisa to Rimini. As part of their delaying tactics the Germans constructed a number of intermediate defensive lines between there and the line of the Arno river. To counter this Allied plans involved the Fifth Army striking out towards the triangle of Pisa–Lucca–Pistoia to the west, while the Eighth Army focused on the area of Florence–Arezzo–Bibbiena. Fortunately for the Germans the advance of the Allies was not as rapid as planned. Nevertheless their first defensive position, the Dora Line, was breached between 10 and 11 June forcing the Germans back to the next position, the Albert (Trasimeno) Line, the Allies running up against that on 14 June. Here they were held in check until 28 June when the Eighth Army finally broke through, reaching Chiusi on 2 July. This forced the Germans to abandon the Albert Line and pull back to the Arezzo Line. Elsewhere, after attacking on 21 June, troops of the French Expeditionary Force took Sienna on 3 July and Poggibonso four days later.

At this point, however, the French were withdrawn, along with some US troops, all to be sent to Naples to be readied for the invasion of the south of France. To replace them the 2nd New Zealand Division was brought in, the advance continuing towards the Arno river, US troops finally reached it on 23 July, while Florence was entered by South African troops on 4 August. In the meantime on 18 July, on the Adriatic coast, the Polish 2nd Corps, after pushing up the coast from the vicinity of Ortona, captured the port of Ancona. Thereafter, the Allies halted their offensive to allow their troops to rest, refit and prepare for the forthcoming offensive on the Gothic Line.

A PzKpfw IV Ausf. H from Panzer-Regiment 26 on the road in Tuscany. It appears to be completed in overall Dunkelgelb. [Jeffrey Plowman]

The PzKpfw IVs in this column, most probably from Panzer-Regiment 26, are completed in overall Dunkelgelb with Balkenkreuz on the side and rear of the turret Schürzen armour. [Jeffrey Plowman]

New Zealand soldiers inspect a Tiger that had been abandoned by schwere Panzer-Abteilung 508 in Tuscany. It would have been completed with patches of Olivgrün and Rotbraun sprayed over Dunkelgelb. [Jeffrey Plowman]

[Right & below right] American troops found this M41 90/53 801(i) in a bombed out railway yard in the spring or summer of 1943. Markings on the vehicle indicate that it was from Panzerjager-Abteilung 51 of 26. Panzer-Division. It appears to have been completed with patches of Olivgrün and Rotbraun sprayed over Dunkelgelb. [Lee Archer]

This Tiger I from schwere Panzer-Abteilung 508 was found abandoned by British troops around the beginning of June 1944. It would have been completed with patches of Olivgrün and Rotbraun sprayed over Dunkelgelb, with white turret numbers. [John Nicholson]

This StuG IV was abandoned after it ran down a bank during the retreat of German forces. [NAMNZ]

During the retreat through Tuscany schwere Panzer-Abteilung 508 abandoned this Tiger. It was modified by 3. Kompanie in March or April 1944 with a boom and hand operated winch on the turret. It would have been completed with patches of Olivgrün and Rotbraun sprayed over Dunkelgelb. [John Nicholson]

[This page] PzKpfw IV Ausf. H, number 834, from 8. Kompanie, Panzer-Regiment 26, was abandoned on the road to Pontedera. With a rough coating of Zimmerit over its turret Schürzen its base coat of Dunkelgelb appears to have been sprayed with large patches of Olivgrün and Rotbraun. The number on the turret was white. [NARA]

Also in the same column of tanks outside Pontedera was this PzKpfw IV Ausf. H from Panzer-Regiment 26. It appears to have been completed in a complex pattern of Olivgrün and Rotbraun sprayed over Dunkelgelb, though not the barrel apparently. [NARA]

The SdKfz 250/9 from Panzer-Aufklärungs-Abteilung 26 in the same column of tanks near Pontedera appears to have been completed in overall Dunkelgelb. The number 50 represents the platoon number and vehicle in the platoon. [NARA]

During an attack by 20th NZ Armoured Regiment on Villa La Sfasciata one of their Shermans was destroyed by this Tiger from 1. Kompanie, schwere Panzer-Abteilung 508. The Tiger was completed with patches of Olivgrün and Rotbraun sprayed over Dunkelgelb, with the turret numbers in white. [Jeffrey Plowman]

This Sturmpanzer 43 from Sturmpanzer-Abteilung 216 was found abandoned by American troops in the summer of 1944. It appears to have been completed in overall Dunkelgelb. [Lee Archer]

[This page] During the battle for La Romola, soldiers from 22nd NZ Battalion captured this Tiger I from 3. Kompanie, schwere Panzer-Abteilung 508. It was completed with patches of Olivgrün and Rotbraun sprayed over Dunkelgelb, with the turret numbers in white. [John Nicholson; ATL]

[This page] New Zealand troops inspect a Sherman III, formerly from 19th NZ Armoured Regiment, that had been captured by the Germans during the fighting in Tuscany and used by them until it capsized. It is still in its original disruptive scheme of patches of SCC 14 Blue-black over Light Mud, with its unit tactical markings front and rear, the Germans just adding the Balkenkreuz front and rear and on the turret sides. [NAMNZ]

Once the Allies had reached the line of the Arno river in Tuscany, their intention was to launch an attack on the Gothic Line, the main effort to be made on the passes of the Apennines. However, with their eyes firmly set on reaching the plains of the Romagna before the autumn rains returned in their full fury, the Allies switched their main effort to the Adriatic Coast, the Eighth Army launching their attack there on the night of 25 August 1944, initially catching the Germans by surprise. Thus in a short space of time they were able to close up on the Gothic Line, launching their attack on those defences proper on 30 August. Good progress was made until 6 September when the attack had to be halted temporarily, thanks to steady rain turning the roads and fields into quagmires.

On 12 September the Fifth Army launched its attack on the Gothic Line in the Apennines, side stepping the heavily defended Futa Pass and attacking through the Il Giogo Pass to the west. Some 12 days later they breached the Gothic Line at this point, outflanking the defences at Futa Pass and forcing the Germans to withdraw to the heights above. At this point the Americans switched their line of advance away from Bologna to Imola, but this soon ground to a halt. They then switched their line of advance back to Bologna, but little progress was made here and their attacks eventually stalled at the end of October.

On 15 September the Eighth Army renewed their attack on the Adriatic and on 19 September had taken both Rimini and crossed the Marecchia river. Unfortunately, having finally reached the plains of the Romagna, the autumn rains arrived in force, swelling the rivers and flooding the roads and plains, thus considerably reducing their pace of advance. The town of Forli was eventually taken on 30 October and Faenza on 17 December. By the end of the year, with snow starting to fall, the attack of the Eighth Army ground to a halt as the Germans established their defences along the line of the Senio river.

This StuG M42 mit 75/18 850(i), number 224, of 278. Infanterie-Division, was photographed on the Adriatic Coast in 1944. It appears to be completed with patches of Oliv-grün and Rotbraun sprayed over Dunkelgelb, with the turret numbers 224 in red outlined with white. [NAC]

[Previous page & right] Nashorn, number 214, was captured by Polish 4th Armoured Regiment "Scorpion" on 19 August 1944 in the vicinity of Vicinato. It was from schwere Panzer-jäger-Abteilung 525 and appears to have had some success judging by the 12 kill rings on the barrel of its 8.8 cm Pak 43/1. It was completed in Dunkelgelb, oversprayed with either Olivgrün or Rotbraun. Additional camouflage has been added by threading wire along the sides of the fighting compartment to which foliage has been added. [PISM x 2; NAC]

Polish tankers repair the damaged track of Colonel Stanisław Gliński's (commander of 4th Armoured Regiment „Scorpion") Sherman III by a StuG M42 mit 75/18 850(i) of 278. Infanterie-Division in Ancona in July 1944. The assault gun appears to be completed with patches of Olivgrün and Rotbraun sprayed over Dunkelgelb, with the turret numbers 232 in red outlined with white. [NAC]

[Previous page] Polish troops examine a Panther Ausf. A, number 214, from 2. Kompanie, Panzer-Regiment 26, abandoned after it ran off the road south of the Metauro river on Monte Rosario on 20 August. It was completed in overall Dunkelgelb, with its barrel camouflaged in Olivgrün and Rotbraun. [NAC]

[This page] On 18 September the company commander's Tiger I (number 200) from 2. Kompanie, schwere-Panzer-Abteilung 504, was destroyed by artillery fire at the base of Covignano hill. It was most probably completed with patches of Olivgrün and Rotbraun sprayed over Dunkelgelb, with the turret numbers white outlined in black. [John Nicholson]

[This page] This Tiger from 1. Kompanie, schwere Panzer-Abteilung 508, was abandoned near Casa Nadiani, over the river Pircio. The Sherman beside it had been under the command of Lieutenant Cross from 5 Troop, 20th NZ Armoured Regiment and had been knocked out on 25 September 1944 by a camouflaged Tiger beside a house some 1,200 yards away. The Tiger appears to be in Dunkelgelb over-sprayed in patches of Rotbraun and Olivgrün and with a hollow white number 1. [PISM; Jeffrey Plowman; John Nicholson]

This Tiger I from 1, Kompanie, schwere Panzer-Abteilung 508, was found by New Zealand troops during the fighting on the Adriatic Coast. It would most probably be completed in overall Dunkelgelb oversprayed with Olivgrün and Rotbraun, and with a white turret number. [Jeffrey Plowman]

On the night of 15 September Tiger I, number 314, from schwere Panzer-Abteilung 504 of Unteroffizier Jobst dropped into a muddy ditch near the Marano river. Shortly after Tiger 324 of Feldwebel Beck slipped in behind it. Both could not be recovered and were blown up. Tiger 314 was completed in Dunkelgelb, with its barrel camouflaged in Olivgrün and Rotbraun, with white numbers outlined in black.

New Zealand soldiers inspect a Panther Ausf. A from Panzer-Regiment 26 in the vicinity of Rimini. It appears to be completed in overall Dunkelgelb. At least one number, 2, is visible on the turret close to the mantlet, suggesting that this tank was from 2. Kompanie. [Jock Montgomery]

This StuG III Ausf. G was found abandoned on the Adriatic section of the Gothic Line by New Zealand troops. It appears to be completed in overall Dunkelgelb. [Jock Montgomery]

While operating with 26. Panzer-Division, this Jagdpanzer IV was abandoned near Riccione. It appears to be completed with patches of Olivgrün and Rotbraun sprayed over Dunkelgelb, with two kill rings on the barrel. [Jock Montgomery]

Abandoned in the Monte Belvedere area between late 1944 and early 1945, this Sturmhaubitze III most probably was from Sturmgeschütz-Brigade 914. It appears to have been completed in Dunkelgelb oversprayed with Olivgrün. [Marco Dalmonte]

This M43 mit 105/34 853(i) abandoned in Ficarolo was from 362. Grenadier-Division. Though its camouflage is hard to discern under the dust and mud it appears to be completed in the factory scheme of Olivgrün and Rotbraun sprayed over Dunkelgelb with its divisional insignia on the transmission armour. [Jeffrey Plowman]

Indian troops inspect the StuG M42 mit 75/18 850(i) in Forli in late 1944. It is completed in its factory scheme of Olivgrün and Rotbraun sprayed over Dunkelgelb. The numbers are red outlined in white. [IWM]

This StuG M42 mit 75/34 851(i) from Panzerjäger-Abteilung 171 of 71. Infanterie-Division was abandoned after it sank up to the top run of its tracks in some muddy ground. It appears to be completed with patches of Olivgrün and Rotbraun sprayed over Dunkelgelb, with the numbers in red outlined with white. [NAMNZ]

This StuG M42 mit 75/18 850(i) was abandoned in Faenza after suffering track failure. It was most probably completed in Olivgrün and Rotbraun sprayed over Dunkelgelb. [Jeffrey Plowman]

Parked in what appears to be a road tunnel on the Adriatic coast in December 1944, this Marder III Ausf. M appears to be completed in stripes of Olivgrün or Rotbraun sprayed over Dunkelgelb. [NAC]

During the winter of 1944-45 the Allies put on a display of captured German armour in the main piazza of Forli. Among the vehicles on display was this PzKpfw IV from II. Abteilung, Panzer-Regiment 26, which appears to have been completed in overall Dunkelgelb. [Jeffrey Plowman]

Among the vehicles on display in the main piazza of Forli was also this Nashorn, finished in Dunkelgelb oversprayed with Olivgrün. [Jeffrey Plowman]

The Marder III Ausf. H on display at Forli appears to have been completed in Dunkelgelb oversprayed with patches of Olivgrün and Rotbraun, while the Semovente da 75/18 behind it is in its factory scheme of Dunkelgelb oversprayed in patches of Rotbraun and Olivgrün, with vehicle numbers in red outlined in white. [Jeffrey Plowman]

[*This page*] One of the tanks on display at Forli was "Deserter", the Panther tank captured by Canadian forces in October 1944 and given to 145 RAC. Covered in Zimmerit it appears to be completed in a disruptive scheme over its base coat of Dunkelgelb. Under British service it had a yellow A Squadron triangle, a white 10 and the words 145 RAC on the turret sides and 10 on the left side of the mantlet. Additional markings were carried on the sloped glacis plate, among them the number 61 in a square in the centre, and 145 in a rectangle on the left. [all photos: Jeffrey Plowman]

Among the vehicles abandoned in Ficarolo was this Marder III Ausf. M and M42 75/34 851(i). The Marder III appears to be completed in patches of Olivgrün sprayed over Dunkelgelb, while the Dunkelgelb base coat of the M42 has been sprayed with patches of Olivgrün and fine lines of Rotbraun. [Arthur Smith]

Also abandoned in Ficarolo was this StuG III Ausf. G along what is now known as the Via Giglioli. It appears to be completed with lines of Olivgrün sprayed over Dunkelgelb. [Arthur Smith]

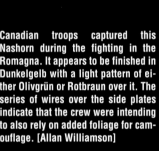

Canadian troops captured this Nashorn during the fighting in the Romagna. It appears to be finished in Dunkelgelb with a light pattern of either Olivgrün or Rotbraun over it. The series of wires over the side plates indicate that the crew were intending to also rely on added foliage for camouflage. [Allan Williamson]

Retreat to the Alps

On 9 April 1945, the Eighth Army launched Operation Grapeshot, its Spring offensive in Italy. After a heavy aerial bombardment of the German defences along the Senio river line, infantry crossed the river in assault boats to secure the opposite bank. Some two days later they had forced the Germans back to the line of the Santerno river. From here they thrust into the Argenta Gap, in combination with an amphibious assault over Valli di Comacchio.

On 14 April the US Fifth Army launched its assault towards Bologna in the Apennines, and though they met determined resistance early on, the Germans were unable to contain it for long through lack of reserves and by 20 April had fallen back to the plains of the Po valley. Unable to hold them there, the Germans withdrew further allowing the Fifth and Eighth Armies to link up at Bologna on 19 April and en-

circle the remaining German troops east of the Apennines. That same day the Italian National Liberation Committee for Northern Italy ordered the resistance movement to launch a general insurrection in the area as the Germans prepared to withdraw to Milano.

Nevertheless, the Allies still found themselves against an enemy determined to put up a fight that continued until they reached the Po river on 22 April. From here, with German resistance collapsing, the Fifth Army thrust north towards Verona and to the northwest to seal off any attempt by the Germans to escape via Austria or Switzerland. At the same time the Eighth Army swung around to the northeast, sending 2nd New Zealand Division in a drive that took it to Trieste on 2 May, while the British 6th Armoured Division struck out for Udine to cut off the German retreat to Austria.

US infantry from 133 Infantry Regiment pass a Jagdpanzer 38 from Jagdpanzer-Kompanie 1305, 305. Infanterie-Division on the Via Emlia east of Modena. It was completed in an Olivgrün and Rotbraun disruptive pattern over the base coat of Dunkelgelb, to which they have painted eyes on the Topfblende either side of the gun. [NARA]

[This page] One of the first tank casualties in the Allied spring offensive was Tiger I number 332 from 3. Kompanie, schwere Panzer-Abteilung 504, which was knocked out with a PIAT gun just across the Senio river on the night of 9 April 1945. It has been sprayed in patches of Olivgrün and Rotbraun over Dunkelgelb, with its turret numbers in white outlined in black. It carries the unit insignia of a black sword and track in a white lozenge on the side of the turret bin. [George Kaye; Jeffrey Plowman; John Nicholson]

[This page] The command Tiger I, number 200, 2. Kompanie, schwere Panzer-Abteilung 504, was abandoned by its crew on the afternoon of 12 April 1945 because of transmission failure. It was completed with patches of Olivgrün and Rotbraun sprayed over Dunkelgelb, with its turret numbers in white outlined in black. [Jeffrey Plowman; Ray McFarlane; Eric Round]

[This page] Tiger I, number 332, from 3. Kompanie, schwere Panzer-Abteilung 504, was knocked out by artillery fire on 11 April 1945 at Massa Lombarda. It was completed with patches of Olivgrün and Rotbraun sprayed over Dunkelgelb, with its turret numbers in white outlined in black. [Jeffrey Plowman; IWM]

[This page] The crew of Tiger I, number 331, 3. Kompanie, schwere Panzer-Abteilung 504, abandoned it after it suffered track damage from artillery fire. It was completed with patches of Olivgrün and Rotbraun sprayed over Dunkelgelb, with its turret numbers in white outlined in black. [John Nicholson]

[This page & above right] Tiger I, number 212, 2. Kompanie, schwere Panzer-Abteilung 504, was knocked out by a Sherman Firefly tank from C Squadron, 20th NZ Armoured Regiment, while trying to escape back through Massa Lombarda, its 88 mm gun having been pushed out of carriage during its attempted escape. It was completed with patches of Olivgrün and Rotbraun sprayed over Dunkelgelb, with its turret numbers in white outlined in black. Standard practice of the unit was for the second and third numbers to be smaller than the first number on the turret sides, but all were on the same height on the bin on the turret rear. [Jeffrey Plowman; John Nicholson]

Tiger I, number 211, 2. Kompanie, schwere-Panzer-Abteilung 504, was knocked out by a Sherman from 20th NZ Armoured Regiment shortly after rescuing some of the crew of Tiger 200. It has been completed with patches of Olivgrün and Rotbraun sprayed over Dunkelgelb, with its turret numbers in white outlined in black. [John Nicholson; Jeffrey Plowman]

[This page] On 13 April 20th NZ Armoured Regiment ran into an ambush involving this Panther from I. Abteilung, Panzer-Regiment 26, near Pallazo Guerrino. Notable is the additional roof armour and the netting around the barrel for camouflaging the barrel with foliage. It would have been completed with patches of Olivgrün and Rotbraun sprayed over Dunkelgelb. [IWM; Jock Montgomery]

[Left & below left] Panther 424 from I. Abteilung, Panzer-Regiment 26 at Sesto Imolese. In addition to its Olivgrün and Rotbraun over Dunkelgelb disruptive scheme, the crew appears to have added netting over the turret and hull secure foliage for extra camouflage. The turret numbers behind the track plates on the turret sides were most probably black outlined in white. [Roy Arnold; Ron Burton]

This Panther Ausf. G from I. Abteilung, Panzer-Regiment 26, was found near the Sillaro river, heavily camouflaged by building wreckage. Note the wire mesh on the barrel to allow the attachment of foliage. [George Kaye]

[This page & above right] This Panther Ausf. G from I. Abteilung, Panzer-Regiment 26, was abandoned by its crew after it fell into a shell hole at Medicina. Like a lot of Panthers from the unit at this time it has additional armour welded to the turret roof to which a disruptive scheme of stripes over Dunkelgelb has been hand painted. Note the mottled disruptive scheme on the barrel, most probably Olivgrün and Rotbraun over Dunkelgelb. When first seen there was additional foliage over the turret. [George Kaye; Lee Archer; Jeffrey Plowman]

On the night of 15/16 April Lance-Corporal John Tucker of 27 Battalion knocked out these two Panthers, numbers 434 and 424, from I. Abteilung, Panzer-Regiment 26, at Sesto Imolese. Both were completed with patches of Olivgrün and Rotbraun sprayed over Dunkelgelb. The turret numbers were painted behind the track plates on the turret sides and on the rear plate, and were most probably black, outlined in white. [Arthur McNeil]

[Above] A Polish soldier inspects an abandoned PzKpfw IV Ausf. J, number 723, from 7. Kompanie, Panzer-Regiment 26. It appears to be completed in overall Dunkelgelb with its turret numbers in red outlined in white. [PISM]

[Left] Both Bergepanthers from schwere-Panzer-Abteilung 504 were lost on 15 April, this one after colliding with a Tiger during the retreat. It is notable for the overhead cover for its driver and co-driver. It has been completed with patches of Olivgrün and Rotbraun sprayed over Dunkelgelb. [Ben Hoban]

[Above right] A New Zealand soldier inspects a PzKpfw IV Ausf. H from II. Abteilung, Panzer-Regiment 26. The tank appears to be completed in Dunkelgelb oversprayed with Olivgrün and Rotbraun, including the barrel. The turret number appears to be 814 in white, the eight being partly covered by the Balkenkreuz. [E. Anderson]

[Right] Abandoned in Finale Emilia at the war's end, this Marder III Ausf. H appears to have been completed in Dunkelgelb oversprayed with Olivgrün. [Marco Dalmonte]

[This page] Jagdpanzer 38 from Jagd-panzer-Kompanie 1278 of 278. Volks-grenadier-Division became mired in soft going near the Santerno river, its gun being destroyed by the crew when they abandoned it. This unit appeared to hand paint their Olivgrün and Rotbraun disruptive pattern over the base coat of Dunkelgelb. [IWM; Jeffrey Plowman]

South African soldiers examine a Jagdpanzer 38 of Jagdpanzer-Kompanie 1278 of 278. Volksgrenadier-Division abandoned south of Bologna. The Olivgrün and Rotbraun disruptive pattern has been hand painted over the base coat of Dunkelgelb. Note the number 2 (as a black outline) between the officer's legs, though whether it was part of a larger tactical number is not clear. [SADF]

New Zealand soldiers outside a casa just beyond the Sillaro river examine a Jagdpanzer 38, number 234, from Jagdpanzer-Kompanie 1278 of 278. Volksgrenadier-Division, from which smoke is still rising after it was knocked out. This unit appeared to hand paint their Olivgrün and Rotbraun disruptive pattern over the base coat of Dunkelgelb. Its Balkenkreuz appears to be white with a grey centre and the number 234 probably black. [IWM]

This 8.8 cm Flak 18 (sf) auf Zgkw 18t (SdKfz 9), "Marder", was from either 1. or II. Batterie of Heeres Flak Artillerie-Abteilung 304 (Sf) which had been attached to 26. Panzer-Division. Though it is a mid-1943 production vehicle its "economy" form fenders indicate that it is part of a batch that were repaired later. The unit had originally moved into positions along the Reno river in January 1945, where it remained until 2 May. It was found abandoned in the Brenner Pass at the end of the war. It appears to have been completed in Dunkelgelb oversprayed with Olivgrün and Rotbraun. [Marco Dalmonte; information courtesy of Nicolaus Hettler, Nuts & Bolts]

New Zealand soldiers inspect a 15 cm Panzerwerfer 42 from either 21. (sf) Werfer-Regiment 56 or 22. (sf) Werfer-Regiment 71 of Werfer-Brigade 5 on 24 April 1945. It appears to be completed in overall Dunkelgelb and someone has painted a topless woman on the inside of the rear door. [ATL]

After the German occupation of Yugoslavia the country was divided up with Italy, Germany occupying northern Slovenia, apart from some regions annexed by Hungary, while Italy took over southern Slovenia, including its capital Ljubljana (Lubiana). Civil control was maintained by the Schutzstaffel (SS) and Ordnungspolizei (Order Police), the latter, in particular, assuming responsible for the strong armed resistance by partisans that developed within a short time after their occupation began. These were organised along the same lines as army units. By June 1943 the situation had deteriorated so much that the Germans were forced to establish two Bandenkampfgebiet or combat zones against the partisans.

Following the capitulation of the Italian government on 8 September 1943, the Germans occupied all of Italy and divided it into Operationszonen Alpenvorland (OZAV), which included the provinces of Trento, Bolzano and Belluno, and Operationszonen Adriatisches Küstenland (OZAK; Operational Zone Adriatic Coastal Land). This latter operational zone included the provinces of Trieste, Gorizia, Pola, Fiume, Friuli and Ljubjana. OZAK came under the command of SS-Gruppenführer und Generalleutnant der Polizei Odilo Globocnik, who was officially HSSPF Adriatisches Küstenland or its higher SS and police commander.

To further support their anti-partisan operations the Germans created a number of panzersicherungs-kompanien (tank security companies) or panzer-einsatz-kompanien (tank company for operative employment). The first of these, Panzer-Einsatz-Kompanie 35, was sent to Bronzolo, Italy on 8 August. On 29 August, 2. Panzer-Sicherungs-Kompanie was formed and dispatched to the Brennero Pass where it took part in fighting with Italian troops on

Located near Milan in the autumn of 1943, these PzKpfw. IV Ausf. Gs, from 2. Panzer-Sicherungs-Kompanie, are completed in overall Dunkelgelb with black turret numbers. [Stefano di Giusto]

10 September. Following this Panzerjäger-Abteilung 171 was transferred to Trieste from Ljubljana on 9 September, only to be sent off to Pola soon after. A further five days later elements of I. Abteilung, Panzer-Regiment 1 reached Trieste and from there were sent off towards Fiume. Finally 2. Pz.Sich.Kp. reached Trieste on 17 September, from where they were dispatched to Gorizia to deal with units under heavy pressure from the partisans. This quickly turned into a large-scale anti-partisan operation that was not resolved until the end of 1943.

In OZAK there were further changes in 1944 starting with the handover of L/48 75 mm PzKpfw IVs to Panzer-Division Hermann Goering, the units receiving in exchange PzKpfw IIIs with the 50 mm L/60 gun. At the end of February, 2. and 3. Pz.Sich.Kp. and Pz.Sich.Kp. 35 were formed into Panzer-Abteilung 208, an independent unit that continued to operate in the area until mid-December when it was transferred to the Hungarian front. Its vehicles were taken over by a new unit, Panzer-Abteilung 212, which had returned to the Balkan mainland from Crete. June saw the arrival of a new unit, 5. (verstärke) Polizei-Panzer-Kompanie, which was based around Trieste, while that

same month an SS mountain battalion was expanded to form a new unit, 24. Waffen-Gebirgs (Karstjäger)-Division der SS, which included some armour in its Karstjäger-Panzer-Kompanie.

A number of these units eventually came into contact with the advancing Allied forces during the final stages of their operations in northern Italy. The first of these was most probably Pz.Abt. 212, which had relocated to the region of the Po river delta. On 29 April, during an attack on Padua, three tanks were knocked out by 4th NZ Field Regiment before it was beaten off. Elements of Pz.Abt. 212 also ran into the British 6th Armoured Division near Gemona, while trying to escape to Austria, destroying several Staghound armoured cars and other vehicles. On 1 May the Karstjäger-Pz.Kp. also encountered 6th Armoured Division, losing one P40 tank to an anti-tank gun that day and two more two days later in an engagement with 1st Derbyshire Yeomanry at Ospedaletto. Finally on 2 May, during the advance towards Trieste, 2nd NZ Division came up against the remnants of 5. (verst.) Pol.Pz.Kp. two T-34/76s being knocked out on the road between Opicina and Trieste and a further two captured in Opicina the following day.

Photographed in Trieste after their arrival in mid-September 1943, these PzKpfw IV Ausf. Hs from I. Abteilung, Panzer-Regiment 1, appear to be completed in overall Dunkelgelb oversprayed with Olivgrün and/or Rotbraun. They also carry a standard railroad-loading label next to the Balkenkreuz on the turret schürzen. [Stefano di Giusto]

In June 1944 5. (verstärke) Polizei-Panzer-Kompanie was posted to Trieste, this T-34 Model 1943 being photographed when it was operating in the Gorizia area that summer. It is completed in a three-tone scheme of stripes of Olivgrün and Rotbraun over Dunkelgelb. In addition it carries a prominent Balkenzreuz on the glacis plate, turret sides and roof. [Stefano di Giusto]

This PzKpfw. III Ausf. N and a PzKpfw IV Ausf. E (modernised with 40-cm tracks), from 1. Kompanie, Panzer-Abteilung 208, in the town of Cuorgne (north of Turin), had recently taken part an anti-partisan operation with some Italian Bersaglieri during the summer of 1944. They appear to be completed in overall Dunkelgelb, possibly oversprayed with Olivgrün and/or Rotbraun. [Stefano di Giusto]

These PzKpfw III Ausf. N tanks from Panzer-Abteilung 212, lined up after their capture near the Po river, are completed in a variety of two or three-tone schemes of Olivgrün and Rotbraun over Dunkelgelb. [Lee Archer]

A PzKpfw IV Ausf. H, number 415, of 4. Kompanie, Panzer-Regiment 1, passing through Sežana to the northeast of Trieste, appears to be completed in overall Dunkelgelb oversprayed with Olivgrün and/or Rotbraun, with turret numbers in white. [Stefano di Giusto]

After their arrival in Trieste on 17 September 1943, these tanks from 3. Panzer-Sicherungs-Kompanie set out for Gorizia, this photograph being taken on the coastal road a few kilometres from Trieste. The PzKpfw IIIs in the column appear to be completed in overall Dunkelgelb with turret numbers in red or black. [Stefano di Giusto]

A PzKpfw IV Ausf. F and a PzKpfw III Ausf. N from 1. Kompanie, Panzer-Abteilung 208, in the village of Ceres (north-west of Turin) during an anti-partisan operation in early July 1944. They both appear to be completed in overall Dunkelgelb. [Stefano di Giusto]

Another T-34 Model 1943 from 5. (ver-stärke) Polizei-Panzer-Kompanie was encountered by B Squadron, 20th NZ Armoured Regiment, on the road into Trieste on 2 May 1945, to whom they tried to surrender. It is completed in a three-tone scheme of Olivgrün and Rotbraun over Dunkelgelb, with a small Balkenzreuz and number 01 on the turret. [Keith Jarman]

After the war this T-34 Model 1943 from 5. (verstärke) Polizei-Panzer-Kompanie was found abandoned east of Trieste near Lipica. It is completed in a three-tone scheme of Olivgrün and Rotbraun over Dunkelgelb, with a small Balkenzreuz and the number 07 on the turret. [Stefano di Giusto]

Around May 1944, 2. Kompanie, Panzer-Abteilung 208, took part in an anti-partisan operation in the Gorizia area. Among the tanks taking part was this PzKpfw III Ausf. N, number 213, completed in overall Dunkelgelb with black turret numbers. [Stefano di Giusto]

This PzKpfw III Ausf. N, number 301, along with the rest of 3. Panzer-Sicherungs-Kompanie, was based in the village of Podgrad (between Trieste and Rijeka) during the winter of 1943-44. The tank is completed in overall Dunkelgelb and carries its unit insignia on the front superstructure plate, the Gemsbock (chamois buck). In April 1944 it became 2. Kompanie, Panzer-Abteilung 208. [Stefano di Giusto]

Officers from 1st Derbyshire Yeomanry examine the P40 from the Karstjäger-Panzer-Kompanie knocked out near Ospedaletto on 3 May 1945. It was completed in the Italian factory scheme of Dunkelgelb oversprayed with patches of Rotbraun and Olivgrün.

[Previous page] In the summer of 1944, I. Bataillon SS Polizei-Regiment Bozen took part in an anti-partisan operation in the Istria. Among the armour in their unit were a number of Panzerspähwagen AB41 201(i) armoured cars, all of which were completed in a three-tone scheme of stripes of Olivgrün and Rotbraun sprayed over Dunkelgelb. [Jeffrey Plowman]

This was one of the two PzKpfw P40 737(i) tanks from Karstjäger-Panzer-Kompanie lost in combat with Shermans from 1st Derbyshire Yeomanry near Ospedoletto on 3 May 1945. The tank was completed in an Italian factory in a three-tone scheme, Dunkelgelb over-sprayed in patches of Rotbraun and Olivgrün. [Jeffrey Plowman]

On 3 May 1945 the Karstjäger-Panzer-Kompanie lost two PzKpfw P40 737(i) tanks in combat with Shermans from 1st Derbyshire Yeomanry near Ospedoletto (near Gemona north of Udine), among them number 111. This tank was completed in an Italian factory in a three-tone scheme, Dunkelgelb over-sprayed in patches of Rotbraun and Olivgrün. The turret number 111 is probably red outlined in white. [Jeffrey Plowman]

Another Italian P40, turret number 121, was abandoned by the Karstjäger-Panzer-Kompanie in Hermagor, Austria between 8 and 10 May 1943. It was completed in an Italian factory in a three-tone scheme, Dunkelgelb oversprayed in patches of Rotbraun and Olivgrün. The turret number 121 is probably red outlined in white. [TMB]

This P40, found in a vehicle dump, was most probably from 10. or 12. Polizei-Panzer-Kompanie. It was completed in its original factory scheme of Dunkelgelb oversprayed with patches of Rotbraun and Olivgrün. Note the Balkenkreuz on the turret sides and front plate. [Marco Dalmonte]

This Italian P40 in a vehicle dump in Verona after the war, most probably belonging to 10. or 12. Polizei-Panzer-Kompanie, was completed in its original factory scheme of Dunkelgelb oversprayed with patches of Rotbraun and Olivgrün. The Jagdpanzer 38 beside it was finished in a hand painted scheme of Rotbraun and Olivgrün over Dunkelgelb. [Marco Dalmonte]

One of the other vehicles photographed in the vehicle dump in Verona was this Panzerspähwagen AB41 201(i) armoured car. It was completed in Dunkelgelb oversprayed with patches of Rotbraun and Olivgrün. [Marco Dalmonte]

Color Plates

M42 75/34 851(i), number 122, from Panzerjäger-Abteilung 171 of 71. Infanterie-Division. It was completed in patches of Olivgrün and Rotbraun sprayed over Dunkelgelb. The numbers were in black outlined in white while the Balkenkreuz was black.

Panzerspähwagen AB41 201(i) armoured car found at a vehicle dump in Verona post-war. It is completed in Dunkelgelb oversprayed with patches of Rotbraun and Olivgrün, with a Balkenkreuz black outlined in white.

PzKpfw P40 737(i), number 121, from Karstjäger-Panzer-Kompanie in Hermagor, Austria, between 8 and 10 May 1945. It was completed in an Italian factory of a three-tone scheme consisting of Dunkelgelb overpainted in patches of Rotbraun and Olivgrün. The Balkenkreuz was black outlined in white, while the turret number was probably red outlined in white.

T-34 Model 1943, number 01, from 5. (verstärke) Polizei-Panzer-Kompanie encountered by New Zealand troops on the coast road into Trieste on 2 May 1945. Apart from the addition of two lockers on the left hull side it is as per factory-issue. It was completed in a three-tone scheme of Olivgrün and Rotbraun over Dunkelgelb, with a Balkenzreuz on the turret (black centre with red lines outside) and the turret number was black, outlined with white.

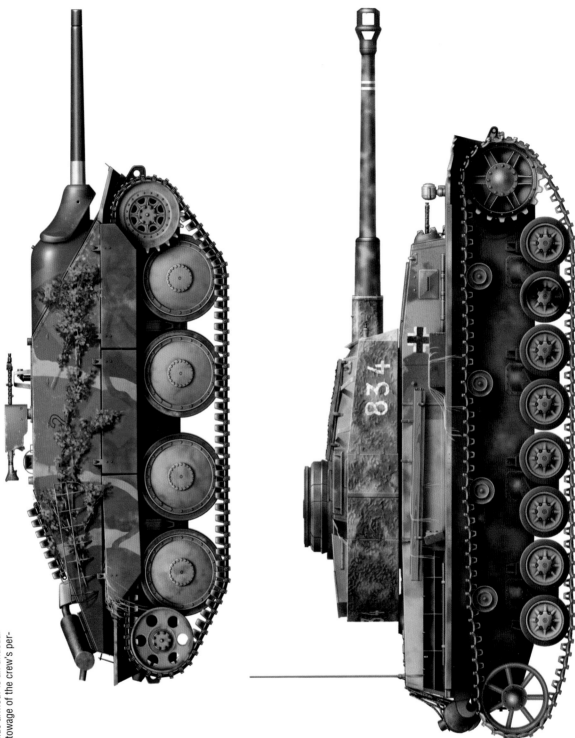

Jagdpanzer 38 Hetzer from Jagdpanzer-Kompanie 1278, 278. Volksgrenadier-Division, south of Bologna in April 1945. It was completed in a disruptive scheme of Olivgrün and Rotbraun painted by hand over the base coat of Dunkelgelb. It carried the number 2 (as a black outline) on the hull side. The rack to the rear on the sloping side armour is an unusual addition, possibly for the stowage of the crew's personal kit.

Above & right PzKpfw IV Ausf. H, number 834, from 8. Kompanie, Panzer-Regiment 26 on the road to Pontedera, Tuscany in the summer of 1944. The Zimmerit anti-magnetic coating appears to have been crudely applied over its turret Schürzen. Patches of Olivgrün and Rotbraun have been sprayed over its base coat of Dunkelgelb and the identification number crudely applied in white on the turret schürzen sides and rear. The Balkenkreuz was black outlined in white.

Left & below SdKfz 164 Nashorn, number 214, captured by 2nd Squadron of the Polish 4th Armoured Regiment "Scorpion" on 19 August 1944 in the vicinity of Vicinato. It was from schwere-Panzerjäger-Abteilung 525 and appears to have had some success judging by the 12 kill rings on the barrel of its 8.8 cm PaK 43/1. It was completed in Dunkelgelb, oversprayed with with patches of Olivgrün, with the numbers in red on the side and front plates. Wire on the side armour and gun barrel has been added for the attachment of foliage for additional camouflage.

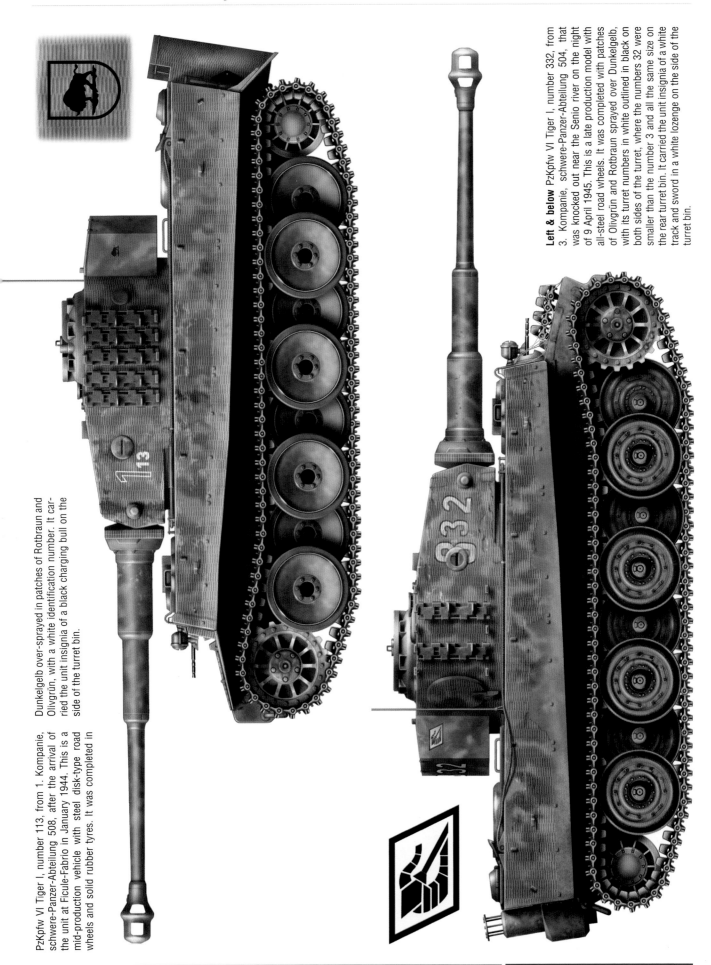

PzKpfw VI Tiger I, number 113, from 1. Kompanie, schwere-Panzer-Abteilung 508, after the arrival of the unit at Ficule-Fabrio in January 1944. This is a mid-production vehicle with steel disk-type road wheels and solid rubber tyres. It was completed in Dunkelgelb over-sprayed in patches of Rotbraun and Olivgrün, with a white identification number. It carried the unit insignia of a black charging bull on the side of the turret bin.

Left & below PzKpfw VI Tiger I, number 332, from 3. Kompanie, schwere-Panzer-Abteilung 504, that was knocked out near the Senio river on the night of 9 April 1945. This is a late production model with all-steel road wheels. It was completed with patches of Olivgrün and Rotbraun sprayed over Dunkelgelb, with its turret numbers in white outlined in black on both sides of the turret, where the numbers 32 were smaller than the number 3 and all the same size on the rear turret bin. It carried the unit insignia of a white track and sword in a white lozenge on the side of the turret bin.

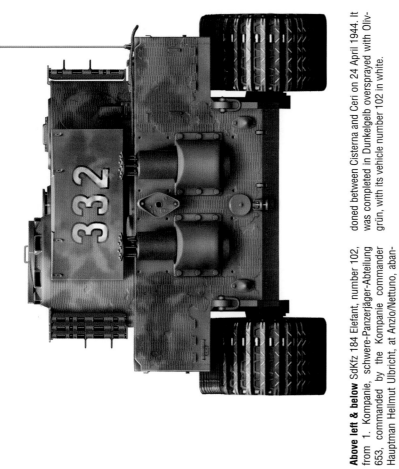

Above left & below SdKfz 184 Elefant, number 102, from 1. Kompanie, schwere-Panzerjäger-Abteilung 653, commanded by the Kompanie commander Hauptman Hellmut Ulbricht, at Anzio/Nettuno, aban-doned between Cisterna and Ceri on 24 April 1944. It was completed in Dunkelgelb oversprayed with Oliv-grün, with its vehicle number 102 in white.

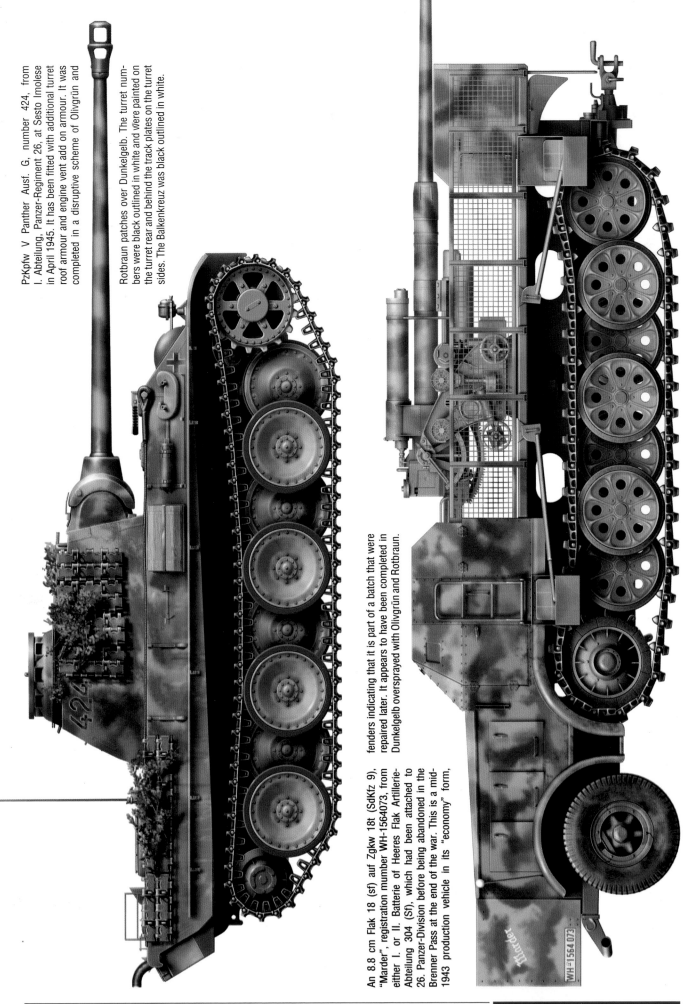

PzKpfw V Panther Ausf. G, number 424, from I. Abteilung, Panzer-Regiment 26, at Sesto Imolese in April 1945. It has been fitted with additional turret roof armour and engine vent add on armour. It was completed in a disruptive scheme of Olivgrün and

Rotbraun patches over Dunkelgelb. The turret numbers were black outlined in white and were painted on the turret rear and behind the track plates on the turret sides. The Balkenkreuz was black outlined in white.

An 8.8 cm Flak 18 (sf) auf Zgkw 18t (SdKfz 9), "Marder", registration number WH-1564073, from either I. or II. Batterie of Heeres Flak Artillerie-Abteilung 304 (Sf), which had been attached to 26. Panzer-Division before being abandoned in the Brenner Pass at the end of the war. This is a mid-1943 production vehicle in its "economy" form,

fenders indicating that it is part of a batch that were repaired later. It appears to have been completed in Dunkelgelb oversprayed with Olivgrün and Rotbraun.